SILENT V

BEFORE it became part of the Severn Trent Water Authority, the Derwent Valley Water Board used to supply water in bulk to the Corporations of Derby, Nottingham, Leicester and Sheffield, and the smaller authorities in Derbyshire.

The history of the undertaking began when the Board was incorporated by the Derwent Valley Water Act of 1899. The Act provided that the Board should consist of thirteen members, to be appointed annually. Three represented Derby Corporation; four the Leicester Corporation; with two from Nottingham, three from Sheffield and one from Derbyshire County Council. The Act also authorised the construction of six impounding reservoirs, four in the Derwent Valley and two in the Ashop Valley. The first instalment was the construction of the Derwent (1902-16) and Howden (1901-12) dams in the Derwent Valley.

First published in 1983
by Sheaf Publishing Ltd
35 Moorocks Road, Sheffield 10
Revised and reprinted in 1989
ISBN 09505458 9 9
© V.J. Hallam, 1989

Ladybower before the waters, looking across Ashopton towards Glossop. Crook Hill is to the right in the far distance.
Derwent Village as it was, probably around 1920, opposite. In the foreground is the Village School with beyond it the Church and the Vicarage. In the distance is Wellhead Farm.

By the Derwent Valley Water Act of 1920 the Water Board obtained Parliamentary powers to abandon the remaining four reservoirs authorised by the Act of 1899 which had not yet been built, (two in the Derwent Valley and two in the Ashop Valley), and in their place to construct the Ladybower Reservoir. When completely filled, Ladybower would have a surface area of 504 acres, a perimeter of around 13 miles and a maximum depth of 135 feet, which would at that time make it the largest artificial reservoir formed by the construction of an earthwork embankment in the British Isles.

After much nationwide opposition, building began in May 1935. 100,000 tons of concrete, one million tons of earth and 100,000 tons of puddled clay were used on the construction of the trench and embankment.

Messrs. G. H. Hill and Sons of Manchester were the designers, with Richard Baillie and Sons from East Lothian as contractors.

Since Ladybower Dam was finished, the gains in water storage have been tremendous, but the loss of the beautiful and historic villages of Ashopton and Derwent have been a high price to pay.

Derwent Village

ALLOW your mind's eye to wander and try to picture a small Derbyshire village nestling peacefully in a beautiful valley, with small stone cottages and tree-lined lanes. To the east of the village stands a Victorian church, stone-built in 1867, from whose spire ring out bells, calling its people together. To the west lies an ivy-clad stone mansion, glorious in the summer sunlight, its gardens in full colour. Beside the mansion runs a river, not very wide, crossed by a narrow, arched stone bridge, once used by pack horses.

Inside the mansion are oak-panelled interior walls to rooms containing art treasures, many with oak furnishings dating back to the twelfth century. A collector's paradise? A dream? Today, yes, but not so long ago it was all so very real; the village was Derwent, the ancient mansion Derwent Hall.

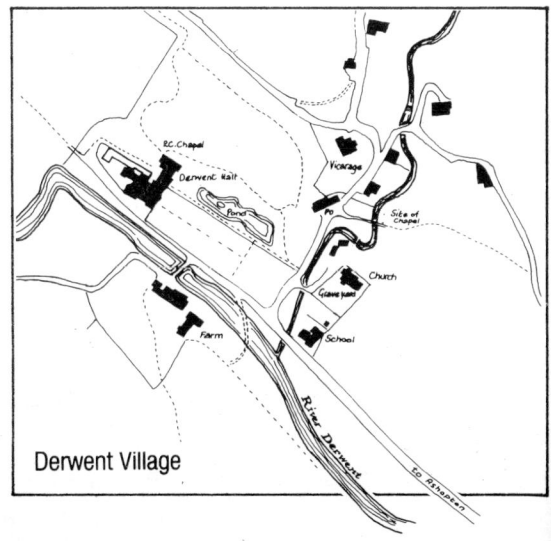

Derwent Hall

THE ORIGINAL part of Derwent Hall was built by Henry Balguy, whose coat of arms and the date, 1672, were carved over the main doorway. A similar carving and the date 1674 could be seen over the stable door. Balguy built the Hall for his son and heir, who was due to be married. The land for the site of the Hall was bought from the Wilson family of Broomhead. Three cottages originally stood on the site, known as 'Waterside', and these were demolished, with some of the stone kept to build the Hall.

The Balguy family date back to Edward I. Thomas de Balgi married an heiress of the Astons, with a large dowry including lands in Derbyshire and Cheshire. The family contributed sons of distinction in both the law and the church from the reign of Elizabeth I onwards. There were Balguys at Hope, Aston and Rowlee. Henry was an attorney and married three times, gaining considerable wealth from each marriage. His first wife was Grace Barber of Rowlee; the second Elizabeth Allyn of Tideswell; the third Anne Moreword of Dronfield. Henry Balguy kept a private bank by storing his money in an oak chest.

There is a story told of a woman who had a strong desire to inspect his hoard of gold. Henry, in gratifying her wish, invited her to help herself to a handful, but the coins were so firmly wedged in that she could not remove a single one.

At least three generations of Balguys occupied the Hall, spanning almost 100 years. The family also rebuilt the pack-horse bridge on the site of an earlier bridge built by monks.

In the chancel of Hope Church, a small brass plate may be seen, commemorating Henry Balguy, who died in March 1685 after - we assume - a very full life.

After the Balguys, the Hall at Derwent passed through various hands, and a variety of states of repair, until in 1831 it was sold to a John Read, formerly of Norton Hall, to the south of Sheffield. Read first furnished three rooms only and used the Hall as his summer seat. In 1833 the lease ran out on Norton Hall, so Mr Read decided to put Derwent Hall in a proper state of repair and make it his home.

In the words of his niece, Mrs M. A. Rawson of Wincobank Hall, *'It had been a nice place to live in former times, but had latterly been used as a common farmhouse. When I first saw it, its appearance was most desolate and dark, and I thought it would be almost impossible ever to make it a comfortable, habitable abode. My uncle's determination and good taste conquered all difficulties and he made it a really delightful residence.'*

Looking across the River Derwent to Derwent Hall, opposite. Halfway up the hill behind the Hall is Ashes Farm, still standing today. The drawing room, above, was extensively oak panelled and furnished with carved oriental furniture.

Most of the rooms had new floors, windows that had been filled in were again opened up. The bare drab walls were covered, some with oak panels, others with fine tapestries, and all the fireplaces were renovated. A practically new fireplace was fitted in the drawing room and when the Hall was pulled down, this fireplace was one of the most sought-after items. John Read also purchased some two thousand acres of moorland and sent invitations to his noble friends to visit him during the shooting season. John Read remained single, as did his sister Ann, who made an excellent and charming hostess.

Soon to follow in John Read's footsteps was the Newdigate family, whose pedigree dated back to Saxon times. In the middle of the 18th century they held the Manor of Kirk Hallam near Derby. The interior of Derwent Hall again had a facelift. More oak panelling was installed, rare silk curtains were hung in all the bedrooms, and an air of grandeur again returned to the Hall. The Newdigates are also credited with the building of the road from Ashopton to Derwent in 1824.

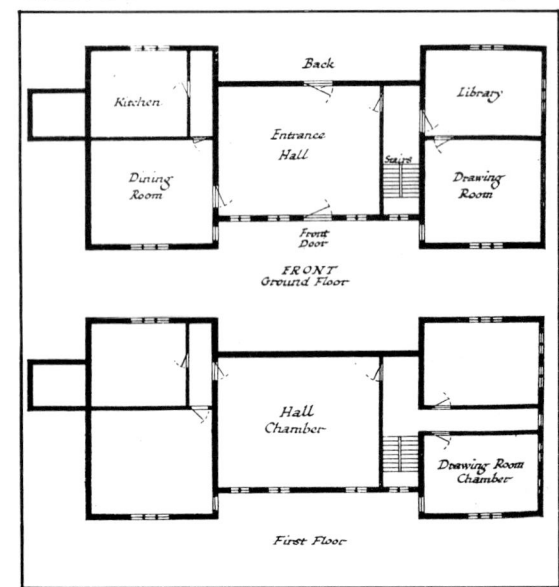

The road, which lay entirely under what is now the Dam, followed the eastern bank of the river, and at the village it turned sharply to the right, whilst the road to the Hall continued along the river bank to the gates of the park. Just before the gates on the left stood the old pack-horse bridge, which provided the only means of crossing the river from the village. It was the ancient bridle path leading from Derwent to Glossop. In 1866 the Newdigates sold the Hall to the trustees of the Duke of Norfolk, and the building was enlarged and a private chapel added at a cost of £23,000. A Roman Catholic chapel was also built above the village.

In a county directory of 1871, the area of Derwent is shown as 3,190 acres with a population of 187 people, the woodlands being 19,999 acres, population of 220. The Duke used the hall mainly as a shooting lodge, and according to many who saw him in the village, he walked around in old clothes not really befitting a man of his status.

From the old Duke, the Hall passed into the hands of Lord Fitzalan, who soon transferred it to his son, Captain Howard.

In 1927, the Hall was sold for the last time, along with approximately one hundred and twenty acres of land. The buyers were the Derwent Valley Water Board, already making ready their plans for the new dam. Oak panelling was removed and for five years Derwent Hall saw little repair. In 1932 it was opened by the Prince of Wales as a youth hostel, and over the following years hundreds of people stayed at the old Hall.

As the number of daytime visitors to the Hall grew, the honorary secretary of the Youth Hostels Association, North Midlands Region, wrote to the Water Board asking for permission to announce that visitors could only be shown over the old Hall between the hours of 10 am and 5 pm, at a charge of 6d which would be divided equally between the Hostel and the Wardens. This proposal was agreed.

Two views of Derwent Hall in 1925, opposite. The top photograph shows the main gates on the West front, with a dated lintel stone over the front door (1672) which was re-discovered in 1989. The East front, below, gave onto an ornamental garden of Irish Yews. At the end of the Hall stood the 19th century private Roman Catholic chapel, shown in this rare interior view on this page.
The early part of the Hall was built in 1672 as shown in the plan, opposite.

Derwent Hall was opened as a Youth Hostel in 1932 by the Prince of Wales. To his right is the Vicar of Derwent, Walter Rouse. Scouts formed a Guard of Honour.

For a time the Hall closed as a Youth Hostel and in 1939 the Sister Superior of the Notre Dame High School in Sheffield wrote asking the Board if the school could evacuate its scholars to Derwent Hall until the Board required to demolish it in connection with their work. The Board allowed Notre Dame School the use of the Hall after an agreement with the Youth Hostels Association.

The school also used the Private Chapel, and one can assume it was a safe and pleasant respite from the hostilities of war which dominated the ensuing years. Other guests to stay at the Hall included (in 1941) thirty children from the Children's Hospitals Association, whose house at Dore had been taken over as a Children's Hospital Annex. By August 1941, the Notre Dame School had decided to return to Sheffield, so again Derwent Hall was re-opened as a youth hostel with a reasonable number of beds held in reserve for accommodating workmen who were employed on the construction of Ladybower Reservoir.

Derwent Hall at that time also became a social

"PEEPING TOM"

centre for the unemployed, who took over the private chapel, and remained for eight months.

By September 1942, the Water Board had repossessed the Hall and were *open to offers* for items. 902 square feet of oak panelling went to Derby Corporation for 2/6d a square foot, along with the oak flooring from the drawing room for £40. Capt. Fitzalan Howard purchased the stone steps leading up to the main entrance for £10 and iron gates for £7.

The Youth Hostels Association wished to buy the special fireplace from the Drawing Room, but the Board had turned down many offers for it and decided to keep it. In its place they said the Youth Hostels Association could have, as a memento without payment, the stone effigy, known as *Peeping Tom* from his place on the stable wall of the Hall. Capt. J. St. J. Balguy, whose ancestors had built Derwent Hall, purchased the lintel from the main doorway bearing the family arms, along with two carved doors. There was a hope that two American businessmen would buy the

Across the River Derwent, opposite where now is sited Bridge End Car Park, a Pack-Horse bridge linked Bridge End Farm with Derwent Village on the west side of the River. The bridge now stands at Slippery Stones, 1¼ miles above the head of Howden Dam.

The stone effigy of Peeping Tom, left, was carved on the stable wall of Derwent Hall.

9

Looking up the Derwent Valley, and glorious even as a ruin, Derwent Hall was demolished in 1943. The remains of the Chapel can be seen, and in the distance is the Pipe Bridge, which still stands.

Hall and rebuild it elsewhere, but this never materialised, so it was left to Mr. Charles Boot of Henry Boot & Sons Ltd, to demolish it, for which privilege he paid £800, taking any items he could use or sell.

By the summer of 1943, Mr Boot's men had done their job. Gone forever was the magnificent old mansion, which, over the years, had seen many changes and comings and goings. One eye-witness recalled looking over the ruins for the last time. *'As the evening sunlight played on the piles of rubble and dressed stone, one still felt there was an air of grandeur about the place, it still looked magnificent, even in ruins.'*

Close to the main gates of Derwent Hall, spanning the River Derwent, stood the Pack-Horse Bridge. When Henry Balguy built his Hall he rebuilt the bridge on the site of an earlier bridge — by then in a very poor state — which carried the ancient bridle track from Derwent to Glossop. The Water Board planned to demolish the bridge, but it was scheduled under the Ancient Monuments Act (1931) as a monument, the preservation of which was of considered to be of national importance. The Board was asked to dismantle and re-erect the bridge at a site just below Elmin Pitts Farm, as under section 17 of the Derwent Valley Water Act of 1920, they were compelled to provide a footbridge there.

This they declined to do. A letter from the Secretary of the Sheffield and Peak District Branch of the Council for the Preservation of Rural England stated that the cost of the removal and the re-erection of the bridge had been estimated by the architect of the Ancient Monuments Department of HM Office of Works at approximately £1,000. He asked the Board for a substantial contribution towards the cost when the subscription list was opened. The Board contributed £50 with an undertaking that the work must be carried out satisfactorily.

The Pack-Horse Bridge was removed stone by stone, each one being numbered before being put into storage at Abbey Grange until the money was raised to rebuild it. The bridge now stands at the head of Howden Reservoir at Slippery Stones, as a memorial to John Derry, who did so much to acquaint people with the lesser-known foot and bridle paths of Derbyshire. If you are in the area it is well worth the walk from Kings Tree to Slippery Stones (just over one mile) to have a look at the old Pack-Horse Bridge.

The ruins of Derwent Hall re-appeared in 1976, when the waters fell abnormally. In 1989 the waters again yielded their secret. The building in the distance is a long-disused stone water valve-house.

Derwent Church

ONE OF THE most tragic losses at Derwent was the village church, dedicated to the Saints John and James. As with all village churches, it was the centre of social as well as religious activities.

As people did not move far from their villages, it was for most Derwent people a case of from font to the grave. Although the church dated only from 1876, the Derwent valley holds a long history of religious worship.

Early records show the acquisition of land in the valley of the River Derwent by the Abbey of Welbeck, by a gift of King John when he was the Duke of Montaigne. It was described as a large territory in the Peak Forest, the pastures of Crookhill, the woods of the Ashop up to Lockerbrook, and from thence up the valley to Derwenthead. The grant of this land was later confirmed by Henry III.

The Lords of Hathersage held land in the Derwent Valley, and on the death of Matthew de Hathersage in 1271 the estate was divided between his co-heiresses, Matilda and Cecilia. Matilda married Sir Walter de Goushill and the couple had two sons, John and Simon. Cecilia married Nigel de Langford and they had a son Nigell and a grandson Oliver. Simon de Goushill and Oliver de Langford gave their lands to the Abbey of Welbeck.

On part of the new land, the monks built an extensive farm known as Abbey Grange. A taxation roll in 1299 valued the Welbeck estate at Crookhill at £7-17s-6d and the tithe 15/9d (cox). Granges such as the one in the Derwent Valley were of immense wealth to the Abbey, and careful breeding and good management gave them large herds of cattle, sheep and swine. In the reign of Edward III the Grange obtained an exemption

Derwent Church, above, was built in 1867 and dedicated to the Saints John and James. The Bingham children stand at the gates of Derwent Church around 1910, opposite.

by the authority of the Pope from the payment of tithes. In the fields they grew cereals, vegetables in their gardens, and orchards full of fruit.

The White Cannons were known for their abstinence, deep piety and graceful dress - a long white cloak and hood over a white cassock with a small white cap. For many years the monks were vegetarians, but as meat became plentiful, the habits of a lifetime changed. The monks also built no less than four chapels in and around the valley.

The first chapel was attached to the Grange itself, and the second stood in the Derwent woodlands close to the site of the old church of Derwent, where they also built a corn mill. This chapel was probably the most important, being close to the mill and water, and a small hamlet soon sprung up around it. A third chapel stood on a site between Marebottom and Birchinlee, and many old maps show a Chapel Lane in that area bearing out the tradition.

The third and fourth chapels - the fourth used to stand in the woodlands close to the old Roman road, about 130 yards south of Hope Cross - were Wayfarer chapels, offering travellers both religious sustenance and food and shelter for the night. If they stayed longer, travellers were given tasks to do to pay for their keep.

The monks never missed an opportunity to gather acorns from the woods, and from herbs they made many fine concoctions and potions. In 1285 the Abbot of Welbeck was fined £20 for damage to the King's woods in the Derwent and Ashop Valleys. Later they were granted a charter for the rights of herbage and foliage in certain parts of the Derwent Valley. Not only were they good at farming, but the monks were good bridge builders too, building one bridge opposite the Grange and another lower down the valley on the site of the old Pack-Horse Bridge close to Derwent Hall.

They continued their happy and prosperous ways up until the dissolution of monasteries and abbeys in the reign of King Henry VIII. The Reformation made Henry much richer but turned many of the monks into homeless wanderers.

One by one the chapels around Derwent began to deteriorate, until only one remained as a place

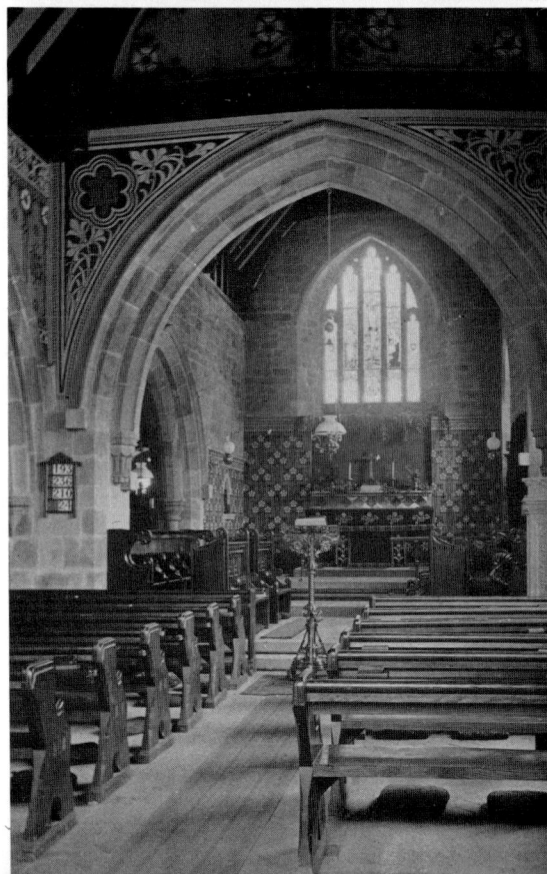

Behind the screens, above, the human remains of 285 people were removed from Derwent Churchyard in 1940. Each exhumation was carefully recorded, but not always did the gravestone details agree with the exhumed contents.
The church interior was photographed long before there were any serious plans to flood the valley.

REMOVAL OF HUMAN REMAINS FROM DERWENT CHURCHYARD.
RECORD SHEET.

					SKETCH OF MONUMENT (if any)	INSCRIPTION ON MONUMENT (if any)
1.	Number of Original Grave on Plan of Derwent Churchyard.	B. 8. 58.				Eliza. wife of Daniel Edwards. of Pontrhydyrun, Monmouthshire. died Oct. 19th 1903. aged 68 years. Also of Daniel Edwards, husband of the above. died Jan. 26th 1913. also Daniel George son of the above died Sept 18th 1918. aged 52 years.
2.	Number of Bodies or remains exhumed.	Three				
3.	Particulars of Monument edge, or tombstone (if any). (Detailed sketch to be made before removal of Monument and attached hereto.)	Stone Headpiece Kerbs. Footstone.				
4.	Date of removal of Monument, edge, or tombstone.	24 April 1940				
5.	Date of re-fixing of Monument, edge, or tombstone.	22 August 1940				
6.	Names of Persons interred in original Grave.	Daniel George Edwards.	Daniel Edwards.	Eliza Edwards.		
7.	Date and time of exhumation.	29th May 1940. 2 p.m.	29th May 1940. 3.30 p.m.	29th May 1940. 4.30 p.m.		
8.	Depth of remains below surface of ground.	3'-6".	5'-6".	7'-6".		
9.	Nature of subsoil at level of remains.	Bind.	Bind.	Bind.		
10.	Condition of coffin (if any).	bad.	bad.	bad.		
11.	Condition of remains.	complete skeleton.	complete skeleton.	complete skeleton.		
12.	Persons present at exhumation.	Mr J. Heath.	Mr J. Heath.	Mr J. Heath.		
13.	Number of Grave on Plan of Bamford Churchyard where remains re-interred.	~~30.~~ 41.	~~30.~~ 41.	~~30.~~ 41.		
14.	Date and time of re-interment.	30th May 1940. 11. a.m.	30th May 1940. 11. a.m.	30th May 1940. 11. a.m.		
15.	Persons present at re-interment.	Mr J. Heath.	Mr J. Heath.	Mr J. Heath.		

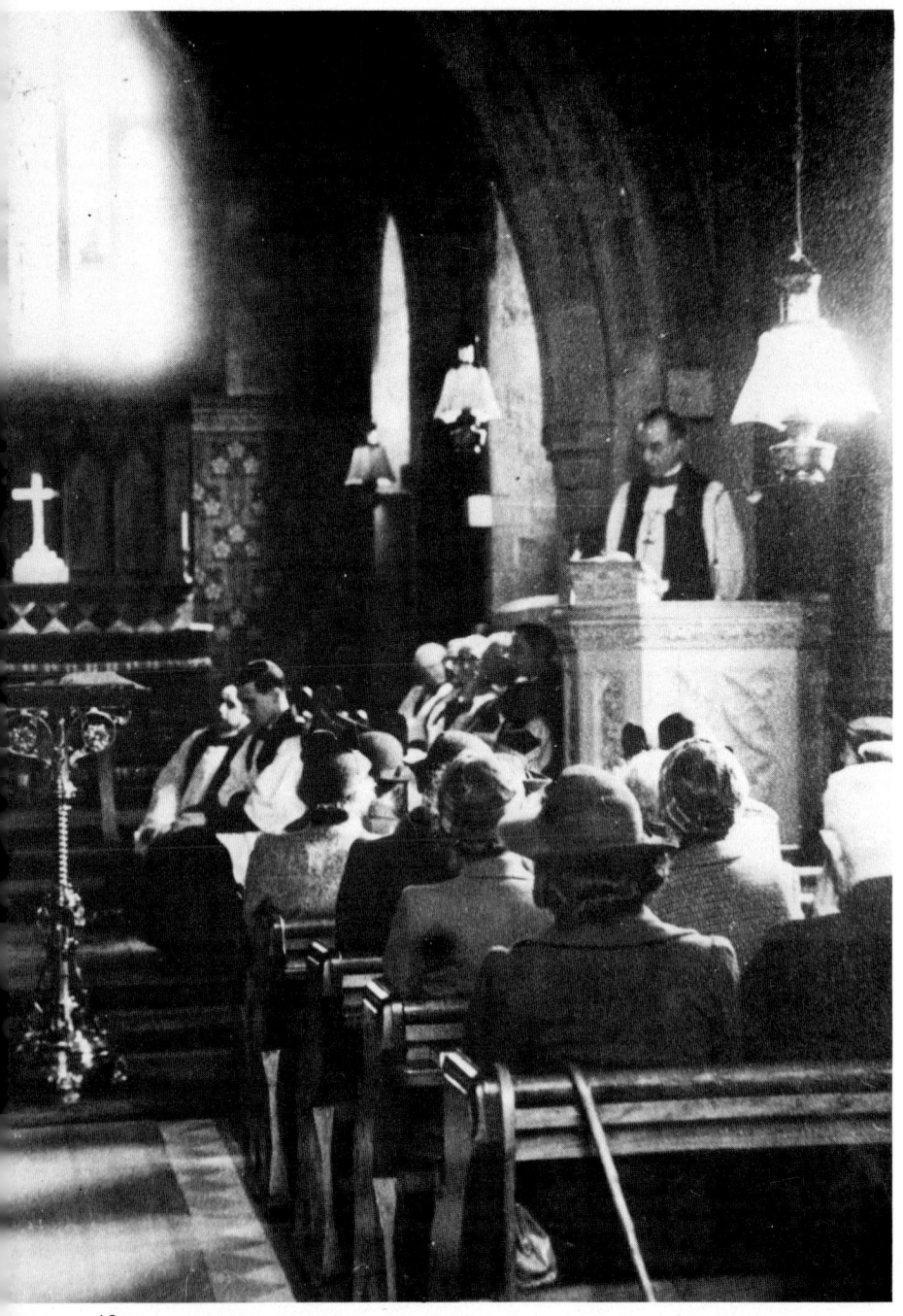

of, by then Protestant, religious worship. It continued thus until 1757. In 1688, the Earl of Devonshire owned the corn mill at Derwent and pastured sheep at Derwent Woodlands. He paid, through his agent, Mr Greaves of Rowlee, a gratuity of five pounds to the Rev. Mr Nicholls for his services at Derwent mhapel, which had become a chapel-of-ease to the Parish of Hathersage. When the old chapel was pulled down, it made way for a smaller second chapel in 1757, said to have been an ugly building with a square bell tower, containing one bell, with below it a large round-headed window at the west end. After this second chapel was removed in 1867, the church so many people still remember was built. As they were pulling down the 1757 chapel, fragments of the fourteenth century building were found embedded in the masonry, including mouldings, pillars, capitals and window sills. These were used on the building of the 1867 church.

Derwent Church was an excellently proportioned building, consisting of chapel, nave, porch, north aisle with an arcade of three arches. A western tower and spire were added in 1873. The church was consecrated on 18th August 1869. In the churchyard near the south entrance stood a sundial, the work of Daniel Rose, clerk of Derwent in the eighteenth century. The register of baptisms dated back to 1813, marriage and burials from 1869. Other notable items housed in the church included an ancient stone font, dated 1670, which had been rescued from the Hall gardens, where it had been used as a flower pot in earlier times. There was also a silver paten dated 1763 and inscribed *Chapel of Derwent, from Dr Denman.*

The patronage of the earlier chapel had been sold by Mr Balguy to Joseph Denman MD about that time. Joseph Denman was the father of the first Lord Denman. The Derwent chalice of Elizabethan origin was made in London in 1584, and has engraved on it figures, symbolic of the elements.

In 1937 the Water Board purchased the church, churchyard and vicarage at a cost of £18,244-13s, and then rented back the church and churchyard at an annual rent of £120. The vicarage rent was set at £30 per annum.

One of the biggest problems for the Water Board was the churchyard, as 284 bodies were buried there. Under Section 17 of the Water Act of 1920 the Water Board was responsible for both the removal of the human remains from Derwent Churchyard, and their re-interment in consecrated ground in which burials may legally take place, subject to the approval of the Bishop of Derby. As there was not enough ground spare at Bamford Churchyard, the Water Board decided to appropriate a piece of their own land close to Moorland Road at Yorkshire Bridge for the purpose of a burial ground.

The Bishop of Derby visited the site and approved it, subject to the Board fencing in the land, making approach roads and agreeing to keep the burial ground in order in perpetuity. All was agreed, and the problem seemed to have been solved, until it was pointed out that under the Burials Act no new burial ground can be made within one hundred yards of a dwellinghouse without the consent in writing of the owner or occupier of such a dwellinghouse. Only one house, known as Bamford Lodge and owned by Mr G. R. Wilson, was within one hundred yards of the proposed burial ground, and Mr Wilson objected so strongly to the burial ground that the plan had to be scrapped.

At one stage the idea of capping the graves and leaving the bodies in place at Derwent was suggested, but then the Vicar of Bamford approached the Water Board asking if they would contribute to the cost of extending the Bamford Churchard. This the Water Board agreed to do, on condition that the human remains from Derwent could be buried there. The Water Board paid £500 towards the cost, and when the extension was complete, the Bishop of Derby consecrated the ground on Saturday 8th October, 1938.

A packed congregation of villagers, hikers and Water Board officials was addressed by the Bishop of Derby at the last service in Derwent Church on 17th March 1943, opposite. Outside, the churchyard was by then empty and overgrown, the contents of the graves long since removed to Bamford.

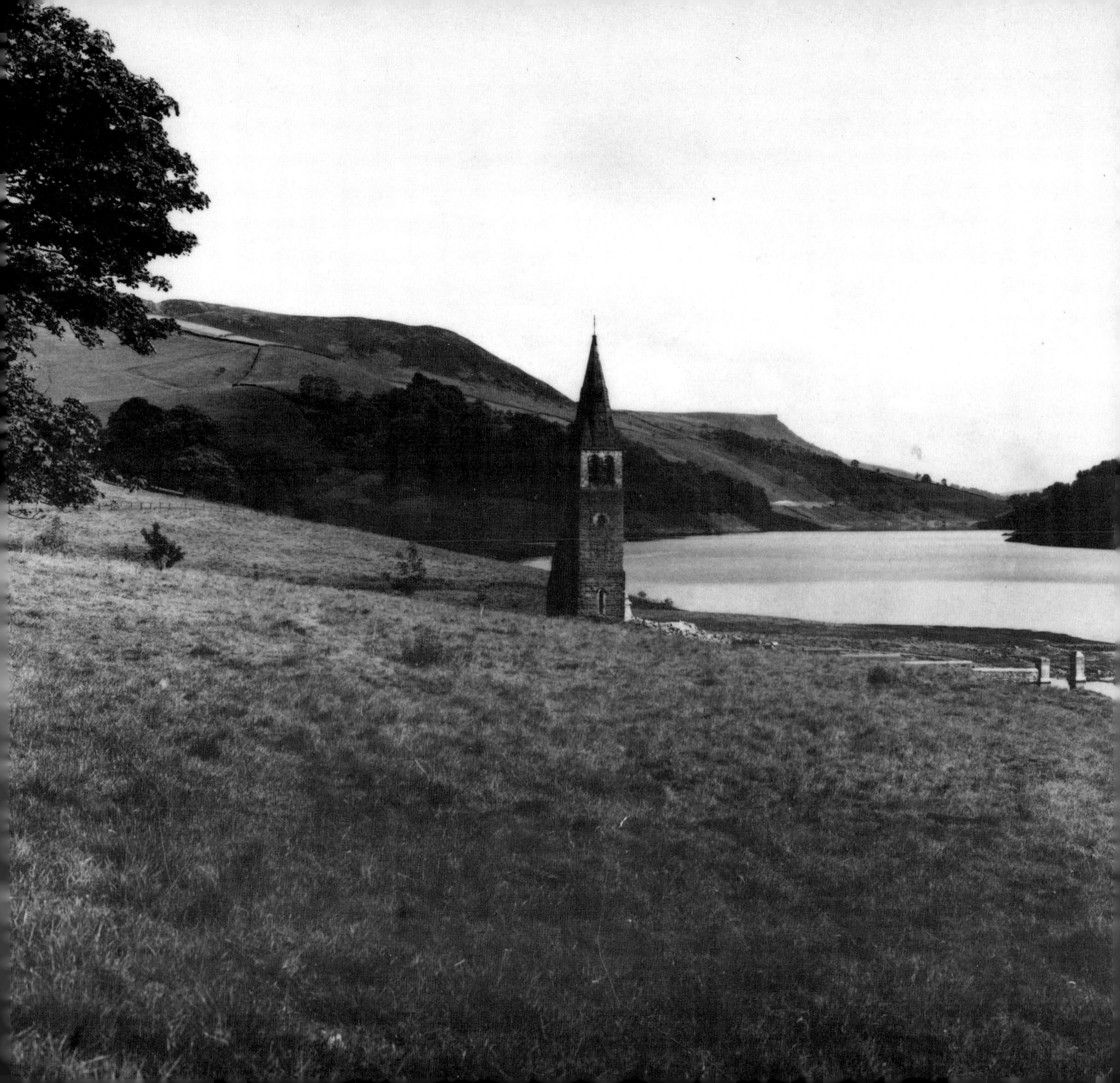

By December 1938, the Water Board had applied to the Ministry of Health with a view to obtaining an Order of the Privy Council closing Derwent Churchyard for burials.

Records of each grave opened had to be kept, and a sketch made of each grave-stone or monument. The condition of the coffin and remains were logged, as were the time and date of exhumation and re-interment. The whole task was carried out under the supervision of the Derbyshire County Medical Officer of Health, who wrote to the Board on 4th July 1940 stating that the removal of the remains had been carried out to his entire satisfaction.

The last service held in Derwent Church was on 17th March 1943, and was attended by the Bishop of Derby and members of the Water Board. In his final address to the congregation the Bishop said, *'We build churches with the idea that they will endure forever, but we know in our hearts that our buildings will not endure, for we have seen so much destruction during the war that we no longer have the illusion of permanence of the work of human hands'*.

Between 1943 and 1945 the water in the silent Derwent Valley rose steadily. The photograph below shows the village in 1944 with the Church, and Derwent Hall beyond it, both in ruins, although a row of cottages and Derwent Post Office still stand. By June 1945, left, looking towards Ashopton, only the desolate spire of the Church and two stone gate posts still stood beside the rising waters.

The pupils of Derwent School, around 1920. This photo was supplied by Colin Elliott who still remembers the daily five-mile walk from his home in Ashopton to attend Derwent School! The wedding took place probably before the Great War, when Albert Shephard of Bridge End Farm married Miss Violet Bridge. The photo was taken in the front garden of Crook Hill Farm. Derwent War Memorial was erected after the Great War and now stands on a new site overlooking the village.

The person hardest hit by the flooding must have been the Vicar of Derwent, the late Walter E. Rouse, for he had been priest there for more than forty-five years. He had been the Board's chaplain to the workpeople when Derwent and Howden Dams were constructed, and on retiring in 1943, he was allowed to continue to live in the vicarage, at £20 per annum rent. He died in 1945 at the age of 81. After his death, the Water Board decided to pull down the vicarage.

After the last service in Derwent Church, the Water Board took possession of the church and prepared to demolish it. It had been hoped that the church could have been rebuilt on a new site, but this proved impractical, so it was decided to transfer the endowments of Derwent Church to Frecheville, to the south of Sheffield, which at that time had only a temporary church. As there was about £12,000 attached to the Derwent living, the Bishop decided that the sum could be most usefully devoted to erecting a parish church at Frecheville, now dedicated to St. Cyprian.

The silver paten and the Derwent Chalice are now both housed at Frecheville. The ancient font, after a spell lost, is now restored to former glory in Tansley Church near Matlock. The four bells from Derwent now ring out calling the people of Chelmorton, near Buxton, together, and the East Window - a copy of an old master - can be seen in Hathersage Church.

The Church fabric was in excellent condition. The pulpit was the work of a master craftsman, and at the back of the altar stood an oak panel once housed in Winchester Cathedral. All these found new and grateful homes. After all the items had been removed, demolition was quickly carried out. The Water Board decided at first to leave the church spire standing as a memorial to the people of Derwent, but as time went on they came to regret this decision.

Also to perish was the school and schoolhouse, for which the Water Board paid £1,000. Also noteworthy was *Mill Cottage*, a delightful house from which Mrs H. Thorp had served many a rambler with tea. Had Mrs Thorpe lived she would have seen her third home perish beneath the impounded waters of the Derwent Valley, for her first home at Ronksley Farm had been submerged under Howden Dam, whilst her second - Hancock's Farm - lay under the waters of the Derwent Dam. But Mrs Thorpe died before her home was needed.

Gone also is *Bridge End Farm*, a 300-year-old farmhouse that had been the home of Mr A. Shephard for more than fifty years. The old farmhouse held an ale licence in earlier times, receiving regular supplies from local brewers in Hathersage.

By the late autumn of 1943, Derwent was little more than piles of rubble. Its inhabitants had moved on to rebuild their lives elsewhere. Many settled on the Water Board's purpose-built housing estate at Yorkshire Bridge, about 3½ miles away, whilst others travelled to many corners of the High Peak.

Lower down the valley at Ladybower, the outlet valves were being closed, and soon the impounded waters were covering the ruins of Derwent. Only one landmark was left to bear witness to the village, a stark church spire standing alone in the cold murky waters of Ladybower Reservoir. But even that did not last long, for it was blown up for alleged safety reasons on 15th December 1947.

Stone from the old Chapel was used on the building of Mill Cottage, to the right. Running right through the village of Derwent was the Mill Brook, which still feeds into Ladybower. Derwent Post Office, to the left, was run by Mr Bingham.

The tower of Derwent Church by 1945, as it was left, right, after the rest of the village had been demolished. In the background still stands the Vicarage and although this was pulled down in the same year, the stone gate posts can still be seen beside the road.
On the 15th December 1947, at a time when Derwent Water was abnormally low, the Church tower was blown up. Much of the stonework has since been incoporated in various earthworks around the Mill Brook.

Ashopton Village in the 1930s, opposite, looking towards Sheffield. The present A57 is elevated and to the left of this old road. In the foreground stands the *Ashopton Inn*, with beyond it a garage run by David Jones. The wooden building next door belonged to Joe Marshall, joiner and undertaker.

Ashopton Village

Ashopton Village

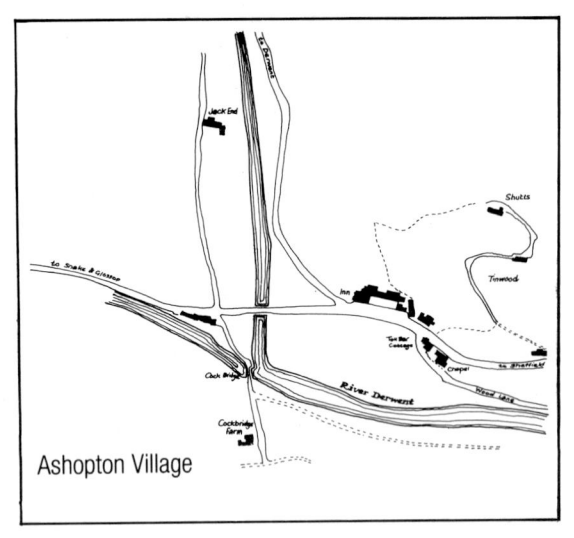

The *Ashopton Inn* was built as a coaching inn, providing meals and facilities for horses on the turnpike road (now the A57) linking Sheffield and Glossop. The Sheffield-Manchester coach stands outside the Inn in the 1880s.

WITH THE fall of the Roman Empire, the roads they had built in Britain were allowed to fall into disrepair. By the Middle Ages they were little more than rutted tracks, but around 1770, following the Turnpike Road Act of that year, roads slowly began to improve, with engineers like McAdam and Telford introducing new methods of road laying. It was these new, surfaced roads that brought about the great coaching era, which reached its peak around 1820.

When the Sheffield to Glossop turnpike road was built in 1821, Ashopton grew and developed as traffic increased on the road, as travel by coach and horse became popular. But coach travel in those far-off days was exacting of both horses and the human frame. More and more coaching stops were needed, for they not only provided a welcome break on a long journey, but food, warmth and shelter for man and beast alike. The *Ashopton Inn* was built as one such stop in 1824, to provide a welcome pause before the long haul up the Snake Valley to Glossop. Standing at the Derwent road junction of the Sheffield to Glossop road, this ivy-clad old building changed little over the years, retaining all the warmth and charm one would expect of a late Georgian coaching inn.

The first landlord of the *Derwent Inn* was William Askew, whose family were horse-breeders and dealers from Tideswell. On 18th September 1925, the Water Board also owned the *Yorkshire Bridge Inn* and the *Ladybower Inn*, and they did look into the idea of rebuilding the *Ashopton Inn* on a new site, retaining the old licence, but as it involved complicated factors the idea was dropped. On 7th January 1943, the Licensing Justices at Chapel-en-le-Frith transferred the licence of the *Ashopton Inn* to premises at New Mills under the Walker and Homfray Brewery, with the brewery paying £500 for the said licence. On 28th January 1943, the Water Board terminated Mrs C. M. Bradwell's lease and took possession of the *Ashopton Inn*, agreeing to make her an ex-gratia payment of £500 in full settlement of all claims. Within a month, the old coaching inn was in ruins.

At the Bamford junction of the Sheffield to

The Toll Bar Cottage stood at the junction of the Bamford and Sheffield roads. Looking towards Glossop in the late 1920s, the *Ashopton Inn* is in the background. The small photograph shows the same spot around the turn of the century.

Glossop road, at the corner of Wood Lane, a few yards short of the *Ashopton Inn*, on the opposite side of the road, stood the old toll-bar cottage. The date 1821 was carved over the doorway. For almost four years it stood on the opposite side of the road and some 80 yards further up Wood Lane, but in 1825 the Turnpike Trust had decided this position was unworkable and rebuilt it on the new site. As the sidebar dealt with people

25

At the top of the Derwent Valley, Howden and Derwent Dams were built between 1902 and 1916. To bring materials and supplies to the sites, a private railway was built up the valley from the Midland Railway at Bamford.

Looking towards Derwent, above, the railway crossed the River Ashop and the Sheffield-Glossop road on an elaborate gantry bridge. Beside the railway is the ancient bridle path linking Bamford with Crook Hill and beyond, whilst the River Derwent is to the right. The line closed after 1916, but part of it re-opened for the building of Ladybower Dam in the 1940s. The present road from Ashopton Viaduct to Derwent and Howden follows the line of the railway for much of the way.

entering from Bamford, travellers along the Sheffield to Glossop road had to contend with the main bar.

All the tolls taken at Ashopton had to be paid into the Toll Trust Office in Paradise Square, Sheffield, with the keeper having to walk there and back — a long, dangerous trip, usually taking three hours each way.

The last toll was taken at Ashopton on 16th September 1875 by the assistant keeper, Mr. Eber Marshall, after which date the toll-bar was given up, and the house sold. The Turnpike Trust had expired and the road became free of tolls.

In 1935 the Water Board paid £1,100 for the toll-bar cottage and sales shop, along with 3 acres of land, and on 16th September 1942, the cottage was pulled down.

Ashopton village housed one of the finest Methodist Chapels to be seen in the High Peak. Built in 1840, the chapel was enlarged in 1896, with the older part of the building used for the Sunday School and public meetings. Before the chapel was built, earlier prayer meetings were held in local farms, usually once a fortnight, with many guest preachers travelling miles to attend the meetings. During the bad winter months, local people had frequently to stand in, and John Longden was one such famous local Woodlands preacher. He was also the innkeeper of the *Snake Inn*, higher up the valley, and many of the prayer meetings were held at the inn.

Two views of the Toll Bar Cottage, looking towards Sheffield. The upper photograph, probably taken in the 1920s, shows Mrs Dakin's sales shop and tea room. On the wall is the sign of the Cyclists' Touring Club. The lower view was taken around 1900.

Each year, about Springtime, concerts were held in the chapel. These were known locally as the Bachelor Parties, for young men in the area produced the shows and provided the refreshments for the many local people who turned out to enjoy these really entertaining evenings.

On 22nd December 1938, the last marriage service was performed at the chapel, on a day which began with a heavy snowfall. All the villagers turned out to sweep a path to Ashopton Chapel, where the Revd Simpson joined together Miss Olive Ollerenshaw and one Frank Booth. Olive wore a dress of rust velvet, whilst her bridesmaid - her sister, Beattie - was in bottle green. The organ was played by her brother, Willis, and the groom's best man was Harold Bailey. Despite the inclement weather, the newly-weds honeymooned in Blackpool!

In November 1936, the Water Board had agreed to pay £2,800 for Ashopton Chapel, with completion of the sale being deferred until they took possession. As people were already moving away from the area, it was decided to hold the last service on 25th September 1939, and this was conducted by the Revd J. Atkinson. The final hymn sung was *The Day's Dying in the West*. From then until its destruction in 1943, the chapel was used as a depot for the local Home Guard.

A sumptuous Harvest Festival at Ashopton Methodist Chapel in the late 1930s, left, and the stone-built bridge which crossed the River Derwent to the west of the village.

There were regular 'Batchelors' Parties' in Ashopton Chapel, when the entertainment was provided by the single men of the village.
Football matches were played on a pitch between the road and the river; Ashopton plays Ladybower in this local derby.

Although part of the fine stained-glass window from the chapel was transferred to Hope Chapel Sunday School, by the summer of 1943 the Chapel was no more. Another part of High Peak history lay in ruins.

Also to perish was *Cockbridge Farm*, built around 1838 and thought to be the third house built on the same site. It had been the home for three generations of the Thorp family. Aaron, the last in line, wrote to the Water Board on 25th March 1937 asking to be released from his tenancy of the farm. He then moved from the district to Ashbourne. *Cockbridge Farm* then became a guest house, the shippan being turned into workmen's lodging rooms.

Cockbridge Farm stood to the west of Ashopton.
The main road through the village in the 1930s, with the chapel immediately to the left, beside the Toll House.

ASHOPTON, DERBYSHIRE. 155.

Looking north across Ashopton, with the *Inn* at one end and the Chapel at the other. The building on the hillside is Tinwood Farm. Aaron Bradbury, left, was the local carrier in Ashopton.

Jack Crapper was the driver of this charabanc which took Ashopton Sunday School to Scarborough in the 1930s.
Outside the *Ashopton Inn* in the 1930s, below, a baker's van (marked Hovis) and brewer's dray are delivering. Across the road, a large sign is being erected, perhaps to inform people of the flood to come?
In the early 1940s, opposite, the huge steel and concrete viaduct was built across the bottom of the Derwent valley. White lines and kerb markings show that this was wartime.

33

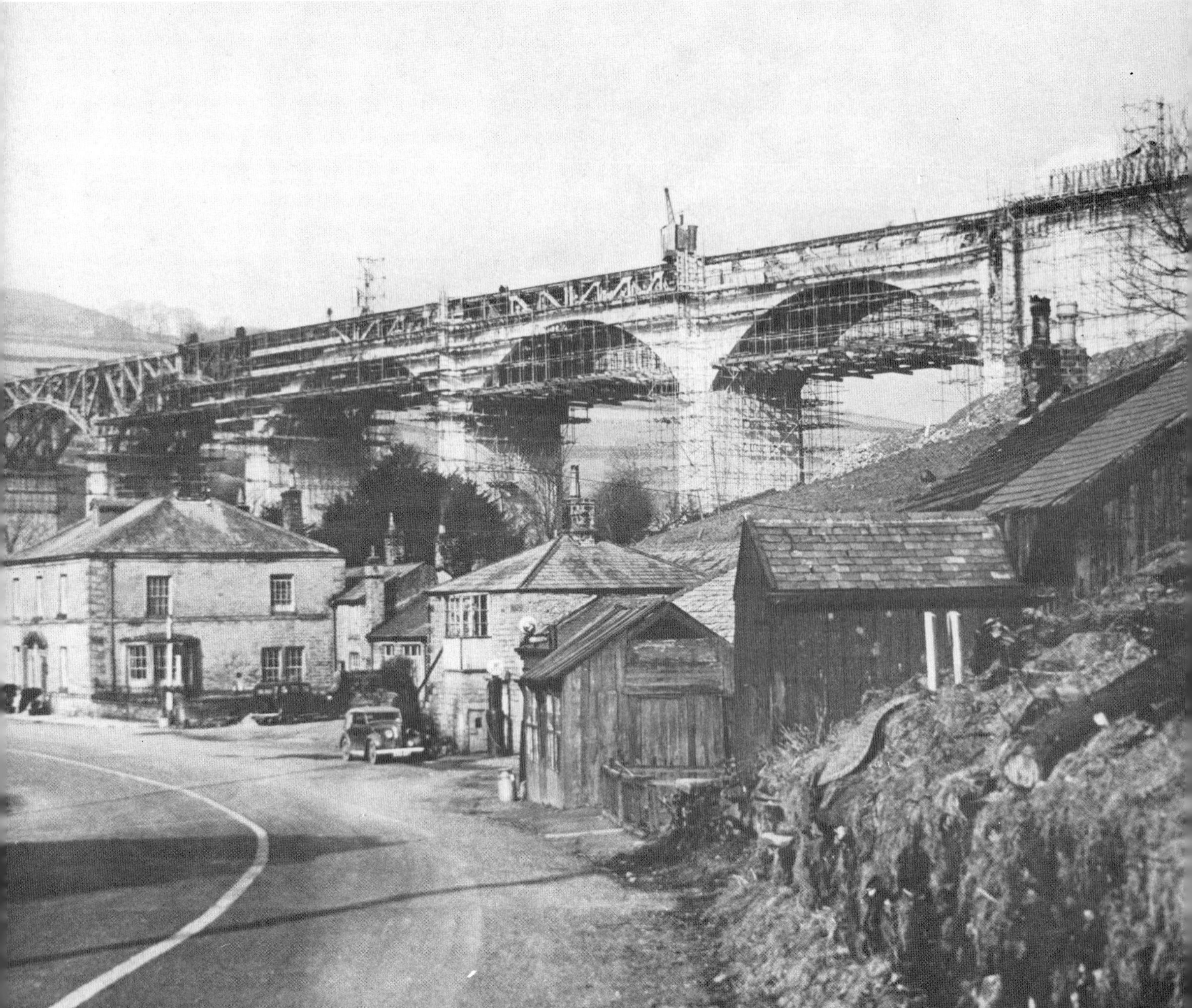

On 1st March 1937, the Water Board purchased *Jack End Farm*, and gave the tenant, Mr T. Bridge, notice to quit, as they required the land for roads, viaducts and pipelines. One of the Ashopton viaduct pillars now stands almost in the old farmyard, for the new section of the Sheffield to Glossop road was built well to the north of the old (now submerged) road.

By the summer of 1943 Ashopton was no more. The inn, tollbar cottage and chapel were reduced to rubble. Shops, farms and cottages (one used to be an alehouse known as the *Highland Laddie*) were all laid low, and above the ruins there now towered a giant viaduct which carried the diverted Sheffield-Glossop road. As the impounded waters of Ladybower began to rise up the mighty pillars, so did the ruins of Ashopton Village disappear for all time, leaving no memorials and no landmarks, just memories.

Smoke still rises from at least one chimney in Ashopton in 1941, although the 945-foot long viaduct is almost complete. By mid-1942 it was finished, and a year later Ashopton was a collection of piles of rubble. By 1945, above, the waters of Ladybower were already rising beneath the viaduct, although the remains of the railway gantry bridge can still be seen.

35

Looking towards Ashopton from Derwent Woodlands. The gantry carried the railway built for the construction of Howden and Derwent Dams.
Although the line had closed by 1914, the piers of the gantry can still be seen today, just to the south of Ashopton Viaduct, when the waters are low.

AS THE years pass, the legend of the villages lives on. Thousands of people visit the Upper Derwent Valley each year and marvel at the scenic beauty of this part man-made lakeland. Many still remember the valley as it was before the waters came, and if you ask them to compare the valley now with the valley as it was, they generally claim that it is hard to choose. But their eyes tell a different story, and often a smile comes across their faces as they speak of the old days, when the River Derwent was little more than a babbling brook, when one could stay the night at Derwent Hall and it would not cost the earth, or how pleasant it was, after a day spent walking in the hills, to rest with a drink and a meal at the old inn at Ashopton. Memories, fine memories.

Beneath the still, dark waters, silt is slowly covering the ruins of Derwent, although there can still be seen the foundations of Derwent Hall and the Church on the rare occasons when the waters are low, as they were last in 1989. But Ashopton is already completely covered with silt. Soon, even in drought conditions, little will be left to see of the old Derwent Village. In the words of a Water Board member reflecting on the loss of the two villages, *'The lines of a picture soften, but they never fade'*. So be it.

AUTHOR'S ACKNOWLEDGEMENTS

Since writing *Silent Valley* several years ago, I felt it was time to bring it up to date and to include some of the more recently discovered photographs of the area. *Silent Valley* now includes the finest collection of photographs of Ashopton and Derwent that can be found anywhere.

I am grateful in no small way to Mr Colin Elliot, who has allowed me to use many excellent photographs from his private collection and also to the following, who helped in producing the first edition: Sheffield Newspapers; The Derbyshire Times; Local Studies, Sheffield Central Library; The Hunter Archaeological Society; The Clarion Ramblers' Association; Mr W. A. Poucher; Mr P. Fletcher; Mr W. Conduit; Mr Richard Heath; Mr & Mrs Frank Booth; Mr & Mrs J. Frost; Mr M. L. Murphy; Mr J. Newton.